Voices from the Sacred Land

Images and Evocations

Lisa Paulson

Thistlefield Books
Plymouth, Wisconsin

Voices from a Sacred Land: Images and Evocations by Lisa Paulson

Unless otherwise noted, quoted material is reprinted from *Windwatch*, the High Wind journal.

Quote by Rumi is from *The Essential Rumi*, translations by Coleman Barks with John Moyne, 1995.

All photos, unless otherwise noted, are by the author.
The photo on page 38 is by Ronald M. Overdahl and is reproduced by permission of the *Milwaukee Journal Sentinel.*

Oil Paintings and ink sketch of trees by Lisa Paulson:
Cover and Title Page: *Prairie Winds Gusting*
Page iv: *Birch on Moody Hill*
Page vi: *Summer Morning*
Page 64: *Quiet Waters*
Page 69: *Coming Home*

First Printing 2008

Printed in the United States of America

12 11 10 09 08 1 2 3 4 5

ISBN-13: 978-0-9816906-0-5

Library of Congress Control Number: 2008903432

Editor: Carolyn Kott Washburne
Design and Typography: Kate Hawley
Production Coordinator: Susan Pittelman

This book is printed on acid-free paper.

A portion of the proceeds of the sale of this edition will be donated to the High Wind Association.

Published by Thistlefield Books
W7122 County Road U
Plymouth, Wisconsin 53073
(920) 528-8488 www.thistlefieldbooks.com

*For Bel, who has always appreciated my need
to connect pen and nature.*

*For all those who, over the years, contributed
gifts of passion, dedication, and strength to
anchor and grow this place we call High Wind.*

*And for the creatures and plants on the land,
who continue to teach us the meaning of balance.*

Birch on Moody Hill

Acknowledgments

The intrepid residents of the High Wind community, whose idealism brought them to this experiment and without whose commitment and talents we never could have made it; who taught me to "see" and appreciate the natural world more deeply.

The Lorian group, whose unique insight as to "how things are" in all the worlds, whose wise perspectives were key in helping shape my spiritual leanings.

The Findhorn Foundation: My visits to this community in Scotland sharpened my appreciation for and sensitivity to all we encounter and work with, especially nature in all its forms—its grand displays and everyday humble manifestations.

My family—Bel, Eric, and Steve—who have indulged and egged on my offbeat quests, each providing invaluable insights and guidance in my attempts to translate experiences and beliefs into words.

To my parents, Scott and Betty Hill, who left me one of the most meaningful legacies of my life—love of the "outdoors."

My editor, Carolyn Kott Washburne, whose cheering helped validate what I'd feared was perhaps a personal, tangential excess, and who so adroitly smoothed out all the sharp edges.

My production/design team, Susan Pittelman and Kate Hawley, who ushered me into the world of publishing and gave me a book that expresses the beauty and wonder I experienced and tried to convey.

Summer Morning

Let the beauty of what we love be what we do.

~ Rumi

Service to the whole remains the motivating driver. To me, this means to each other and the earth, for the highest good of all. It is a transcendent idea that lifts and pushes us beyond our individual selves. It reminds us to walk and feel in the shoes (or hoofs or bark) of all life we encounter, as well as to care for and respect ourselves as essential parts of that divine force.

~ *Lisa Paulson*

Contents

Muse

*T*he idea of creating this book arose while I was documenting the history of High Wind, an "intentional" community situated on the edge of the Northern Kettle Moraine State Forest in eastern Wisconsin. High Wind was an experiment launched by my husband Belden and me in the early 1980s with a revolving group of people who came together to live out some shared ideals and purposes on an old rural farmstead. An adventure spanning altogether more than twenty years, our purpose had to do with a commitment to take care of the earth and try living more consciously in harmony with each other and with nature. On a practical level, it came down to questions of how to build our houses and grow our food. For many, our work also became, in itself, a spiritual path.

As I looked through old letters, documents, and back issues of *Windwatch*, the High Wind journal, I picked out segments that told our story. For the sake of expediency I had to skip over other bits that were equally meaningful to me: descriptions of the land itself, the profusion of natural elements we encountered that deeply impacted all of our lives on a daily basis.

I decided I simply had to write this book to express my own intense love of this land, this sacred land. I also wanted to honor properly what soon became a magnet that over the years drew thousands of visitors. I needed to share the descriptions of the High Wind meadows and woods and hills as we cycled through the seasons and years. People came out to our countryside ostensibly to attend workshops to learn about sustainability and to expand their understanding of life and purpose, both personally and globally. What they really took away were gifts of tranquility and healing and perspective that the land itself bestowed as they walked it and touched into it. It was an experience that we, as residents, soaked up in our daily communal rounds of work and play and rest. Our guests "caught" the same frisson, the same messages from some mysterious deep or over-lighting source.

The bare bones of winter

At first, I was going to isolate a few spare phrases that captured what I felt to be the essence of pure nature speaking: its grandeur, its tiny miracles, its soul-stirring beauty, and evocative sounds— rather like a collection of poems, except they'd be prose pictures. As I riffled through the years of written records about High Wind, I realized what we were essentially about in that experiment on that piece of land was fine tuning our sensitivity to what the land needed. We were about people working *with* nature, not trying to control it for our own transient wants or pleasures.

What attracted us mainly to creating this community was the idea that we as humans are only a small component in a far grander scheme. For every part of life to work in harmony, we had to recognize and live the premise that all life is connected and interdependent. We are inexorably part of nature, which knows instinctively, very clearly, how all its elements function in tandem. If any life form is going to foul up that harmony, it would be we humans, the thinking, or I might say *unthinking*, ones. The ones who think mostly of today and not of how the great earth systems are going to continue into the future.

So along with the land descriptions, I've taken reflections written for *Windwatch* by visitors to High Wind and by the people living here as they went about their work, especially as the activities interfaced with what was going on with the seasonal changes, the daily caprices of weather, the indigenous "critters." Also, it was clear that our lives at High Wind were not only about the land, though its aura burnished everything, but about the buildings here as well—from the broken-down, proud old farmhouse we inherited to the new ones consciously created when the community elected to partner with the nature we inhabited.

The universality of nature's sights and sounds and smells became evident when the experiences I recorded at High Wind brought back precious scraps of personal memories from my childhood elsewhere. I include these as well as part of an important, timeless continuum.

Conversation

*I*n 1990, during an Intensive Journal® workshop held at High Wind, one of the exercises in self-awareness directed participants to think about what energized them, what their passions were, what made them feel more alive. For me it was words, nature, spirit. These were all of a piece, and I wrote:

"Nature is Spirit. Being in Nature is my spirituality. It is there that I can best write and paint, as well as just be in it. It has been part of my life since I was small—having peak experiences in the presence of sunsets, flowing water, rocky cliffs, summer meadows. All my senses are at work, and I also have a great urge to record my impressions and to invite others to share these feelings. . . . It's finding ways to stretch the moment of ecstasy: catching ice diamonds glinting in first light to savor always, remembering prairie grasses blowing under racing cloud shadows. "

The next part of the exercise was to set up an imaginary dialogue with my relationship with nature, which poured out effortlessly into my journal (one of the magical things that happens when writing in this meditative process). What follows is this Relationship speaking:

I was born when you were taken for walks in the outdoors, probably as a baby. I began to seep into your consciousness bringing you to exhilaration, joy. I was "safe." I didn't bite back, I gave you peace and happiness. I began to be articulated through your writing "descriptions" and poems. I was your refuge when human relations became impossible. You escaped to my sunrises and deep forests, you sweated out your tensions on my craggy hillsides. I never let you down. In your teens, I was the catalyst for spiritual revelations that were life-changing. I became the interface between you and your god, between you and your higher self, your soul. I was the place you came to identify with your greatest happinesses, sharing me with lovers and discovering the deepest, surest rudders in your life. I became inextricably meshed with your questing for spirit and fulfillment.

In the Beginning . . .

Autumn 1972

*T*he gigantic barn housed fifty cows until Bel and I bought the farm in the winter of 1970; now it stores alfalfa we harvested last July. The turn-of-the-century farmhouse sagged. Pitted, smoked-grimed walls attested to the previous owners' scrabble just to survive. Panoramic views may feed the soul, but make for lean farming.

Each season in the countryside has brought its own gifts. Last winter, op-art-like, black-and-white contrasts of naked forest against snow, armies of black tree trunks—the bare bones of winter. Black and white Holsteins bunched around feeders. In spring, when we could spare a few minutes from the sanding machine,

Early days: the farmhouse and barn

7

we discovered our entire woods floor white with trillium. Then the birds moved back, nesting in the porch, in the outhouse, under the eaves, making a marvelous racket. Swallows dipped through broken panes to build in the chicken house and swooped around our young sons as they swung by pulley from the highest barn rafters to drop into the hay. We watched for medicinal herbs the farmer's wife had nurtured and used: wormwood by the porch steps as a tonic, peppermint for stomachaches, violet leaves for headaches, chamomile, and more.

Then the new greens darkened with summer as constant mistral-like winds ruffled seas of golden grasses and the purple-blue oats and cornflowers across the road. At night, stars hung lower and bigger than those in the city. This autumn the red oaks and thorn apples flamed as we feverishly tried to keep pace with a giant vegetable garden. With frost, we garnered the last of the gourds, pumpkins, and hickory nuts. Dead cornstalks rattled with mournful finality the end of the cycle.

Evoking a Sense of Community
1981

*J*n 1981, the newly registered non-profit High Wind Association was awarded a small U.S. Department of Energy grant to build a demonstration "bioshelter." Almost immediately the first residents moved out to our farm; from that time forward, Bel and I dedicated it as the base of the fledgling High Wind community—an exploration into ecology on every level.

These early, highly motivated volunteers arrived ostensibly as a construction crew, although very quickly we all realized we were becoming an "intentional community" (defined as a group coalescing around some specific ideals and purposes). In our case, our focus evolved into what Bel likes to call a "three-legged stool": education, technology, spirit. All six bedrooms in the farmhouse, plus the newly renovated chicken coop and cavernous barn, were suddenly filled with singles, couples, and a family of four—about a dozen of us in the first year. We cooked our meals and hauled concrete blocks together and made all decisions by consensus.

Here are my own random observations as well as observations by others as our physical surroundings spoke to us, interacted with us.

May

These weekends are beginning to evoke a sense of community, to be a source of both group strength and individual empowerment. People and nature together creating a center that expresses our interdependence and is a place of beauty, tranquility, and humor. By the way, the first wild geraniums are blooming in the woods just now, and the cowslips are gold around the pond.

September

The summer solstice in June offered a chance for some one hundred High Wind Association members, friends, and neighbors to visit the farm. The day of celebration began when we hiked to the top of the east ridge at 5 a.m. to stand in tall, wet grass watching the far hills layered in flat mists, like a Japanese painting. Gently and rhythmically we shook seed rattles to herald and honor the coming of the sun, which finally rose in red splendor to burn through its grey shroud.

Now, following a summer of cold rains with wild winds that blew over tents, alternating with heat that drove us to swim in the spring-fed pond, the golden shimmer of autumn has begun. There is that feeling of time suspended between strong seasonal assertions, a spinning out of summer, an opportunity at last to reflect on the kaleidoscope of happenings. Time to sit a bit amidst the wild aster and mustard and meadow grasses drying and sending off their seeds. Moments to sense a palpable peace as we step into the cool woods to carry out logs for winter stoves. The pantry shelves are filling with jars of vegetables, fruits, and pickles, and the freezer containers multiply. Bob's bees have given us over two hundred pounds of honey.

The Comfort of Many Hands
1982

February

*I*f any of the new residents of the High Wind farm had been skeptical about the validity of its name, those doubts have been blown clean away this winter. Gathering momentum on the high, open west fields, the blasts howl around the corners of the farmhouse and sing in the electric wires. They've sculpted the already abundant snow into spectacular mountains, nearly marooning the chicken coop, and they have periodically drifted the county roads shut. An expedition to the bioshelter site (designated for our first experimental building, a micro-farm with an innovative passive solar design that produces rather than consumes energy) invites frostbite in the extreme cold. Nature is clearly in charge.

We found ourselves relaxed into the inevitable flow and just going with it. After a tough month struggling with the bioshelter construction, we suddenly had to let go and concentrate on the even more pressing priorities of coping with the snow and plunging temperatures. We began to function as a team once again and got into the yoga of digging out and starting the vehicles and chopping logs for our woodstoves—our only heat. We were focusing outward, adjusting to the demands of the elements, listening to nature rather than to our own circular arguments, and we discovered that the heaviness of difference melted away. The sun came out, along with the cross-country skis and tires for sliding down hills. Our moon boots squeaked more purposefully across the crystalline splendor, and we felt a bit wiser.

Alida, one of our community's first residents, notes:

> It was comforting to have lots of hands to carry in wood and shovel snow. It occurs to me that I have never before known winter's gift, the luxury of slowing down and hibernating. There is time for many things, including storytelling and dis-covering new facets of one another. . . . One of the best parts of winter is that we all do everything, from sweeping snow out of the bioshelter to cutting wood to cooking. . . . Winter has given me time to observe my expectations and to release myself and others from "oughts" and "shoulds." Being snowbound is one of the greatest treats I've been given at High Wind. There's very little to do (by our normal stan-dards, that is), so we amuse ourselves reading aloud, playing games, or sitting around the floor grate mending clothes and enjoying the warmth of the wood furnace.

June

With the melting of the last patches of snow in the deepest gla-cier-scooped kettles late in April, our knit caps were, figuratively speaking, hurled into the air to salute the end of winter. Spring warmth seeped into the earth and our bones, and we exploded out of our pressure-cooker dwelling places onto the hills and into the woods to hunt the first violets and trillium and wild orchids.

Because we were arbitrarily cloistered during much of the winter, our interfacing with the outside world was minimal. So it was with a slightly insane joyousness that we welcomed Kathleen's initiative in orchestrating the spring equinox celebration on March 21. You'll recall that the snow was still very much with us, but sixty brave High Wind members ventured out to the country for a day of, quite liter-ally, exorcising our winter hang-ups.

We scribbled all this emotional junk on miles of ticker tape that we carried up the hill to the bioshelter site (place of the new, of prom-ise), accompanied by appropriate dirges, and gleefully burned it in a hole dug in the drifts. Next, our imaginations were unleashed to conjure up future dreams and resolves that we sent up in balloons.

Tom, who regularly trekked up the hill to record the wind velocity on our High Wind anemometer, was also our resident bird expert. He wrote in his "Aeolian Affairs" column in our journal *Windwatch*:

> The wind at High Wind is mine. And the broad-winged hawks that soar high above the anemometer and the marsh hawks that skim along just above the grass. The meadowlarks, bobolinks and red-winged blackbirds that approach their fencepost perches from downwind when the wind is strong. The barn swallows that glide and swoop on the wind, two of whom are occupying the old cliff swallow nest just outside the kitchen door. And the warblers, nuthatches, sapsuckers, creepers and woodpeckers who are most easily found on the lee side of an esker out in the forest . . . .

During the Indian Institute (a residential workshop where eight local Ojibwe and Menomonee came to teach their native craft skills and share their philosophy), we were roused each morning at 5 a.m. to greet the sun and follow ethnobotanist Lee Olsen into the meadows, the forest, the fen. Lee, who "shines like

Ethnobotany in the field: Lee Olsen leads a walk.

a beacon in life and in his field" (as described by one participant), gave the Latin, Indian, and common names, with the uses and stories behind every plant and tree we encountered.

For instance, we found that the prolific weed lambs quarters contains more B vitamins and minerals than many other vegetables, is excellent cooked or in salads, and has seeds that may be ground into flour for bread. Cattails have numerous uses also: the roots being akin to potatoes; the stalk, like cucumber and good in salad; the stamens eaten like corn; and the leaves dried and woven for mats and wigwam coverings.

Over and over we stood in awe at the wise plan that orchestrates the overall evolving of the natural forest: how, for example, faster growing trees, like basswood, are provided to shade the slower, longer-lived maples while the latter get started, and then they die out to give others room and light.

John Boatman's nightly lectures covered Indian village life and culture, the reality of dreams that link us to the spirit world, the meanings in nature forms. He also hypothesized that "our tree," a crooked black oak in the back forest, was deliberately bent to mark an Indian council ground—over four hundred years ago. After dark, we gathered on the open hilltop to dance and sing and tell stories. We pounded the great drum, with as many as six of us at a time beating in unison. When the fire burned low, we became quiet, sensing the closeness to each other, to the stars, to the shadowy community of trees nearby, and to the wind moaning in their branches. One of the gifts of these eight days was learning to listen to the voices around us, only a few of which happen to be human.

July

Another High Wind event, which happened to fall over July 4, was a seminar called "The Destiny of the United States: Visions of *Inter*dependence." The conversations came together the final day with a "Constitutional Convention," where we prepared a

Declaration of Interdependence. A solemn ceremony was performed in the barn where each of the forty "delegates" strode to a table to sign the final document. It was a gloomy day, and the flicker of a single candle added to the drama. The preamble read: "In order to satisfy life's yearning for love and wholeness, and to guarantee humanity's right to livelihood, well-being and aspiration to co-creativity, we hereby accept the interdependence of all earth's creatures."

August

Tom, our expert on winged beings, reported again after the Indian Institute, this time on a conversation with Coco, one of the Menomonee leaders:

Coco said, "The birds protect me as I walk up the path to my tepee."

I tried to explain that the redwing blackbirds had a nest in that area they were guarding, but she would have none of it.

"They protect me and when I get near my tent I look up and thank them and they fly away."

I have to admit I like her interpretation of bird behavior better than my own.

"Coco" (an Indian word for grandmother) was one of the delightful aspects of living at High Wind this summer through two seminars, a gardening workshop and visits by various groups and individuals. . . .

Of the physical environment, perhaps what I will miss most is the solar shower. [Tom was about to move away from the community.] We got it working during the first seminar in June and I've been forced indoors only twice since—once during an early plumbing problem and once due to the weather. It's not always comfortably warm, but is always environmentally benign. It operates on passive solar principles—no pumps are involved—and is a shining example of our quest for self-sufficiency.

My departure means someone else will be reading the anemometer. The data collected so far indicates that our site is just about at the margin of what is considered an economically feasible wind speed (10.5 mph). I checked at the office loaning anemometers and found that ours has the best readings in the state. That is enough to convince me we should proceed with wind power.

Among the nice features of wind energy is the fact that there is more of it when it is most needed. Actually, March and April have been our windiest months so far; March had steadier velocities in the middle ranges, while April's gusts were in the upper ranges. Since then things have almost come to a standstill. August will be the calmest month by far."

September

Perched on the roof trusses inside the bioshelter a couple of weeks ago, I was plastering the ceiling and noticed it was pleasantly cool and a breeze was circulating splendidly. The building was beginning

BELDEN PAULSON

The heartbeat of nature: beating the drum
at the Indian Institute

to work! Even though not all of the eighteen-inch layer of ceiling insulation is in place yet, it's now providing protection from the blazing summer sun, just as it will help hold the heat in winter.

From my vantage point, I looked south across the road to the blue haze of chicory, then out the east bedroom window to the golden sea of oats in Alida's field, and over tiers of green hills to the Sheboygan skyline poking up on the horizon twenty miles away that marks Lake Michigan's shore.

Later that night, I trekked up the hill to the bioshelter again. I wanted to experience the starry canopy through the southern expanse of greenhouse glass, sitting quietly in the observatory-like living room. A warm wind then beckoned me out onto the great grassy dome of hill behind.

I sat there in the circle where a month before during the Indian Institute we had gathered each evening to chant and dance around the fire and beat the big drum. The beat was meant to res-onate with the pulsing of nature which, if we tuned in, we could begin to feel within our own beings, and which got into our feet and set us stomping. I could hear it now, reverberating in my memory, and I got up to dance in the silence with only the dark sky watching.

Some kind of inspired prompting must have made us choose this evocative location—a site, indeed, to lift the souls of those who will live and meet and work here. The bioshelter itself will become part of the mysterious, ongoing environmental cycles. It will be an instrument to link the rhythms of nature, both inside and outside.

The Vision Made Manifest

1983

May

We're not unaware that the catalyst bringing people to High Wind is somewhat different from that of many communities formed around a particular philosophical idea or spiritual practice. All of us are deeply spiritual in sometimes unspoken ways. My personal feelings about God have to do with a broader interpretation than in most traditional religions. To me, the intricacies and elegance of nature are constantly showing us the mind of an ultimate intelligence at work.

The sacred intent of High Wind was spelled out clearly from the beginning, yet it is the physical "form-level" projects, starting with the bioshelter, that are the principle magnets drawing some of us. Our task, as the bioshelter nears completion, is to work more consciously to integrate our highest visions with the powerful energy that our physical projects elicit at the other end of the spectrum. This means strengthening our "middle," or the "glue," that connects these two, which in turn will define the being of High Wind as growing toward wholeness and stature.

Like the violets poking up now through a brown mat of leaves in the woods, High Wind is emerging, like clockwork, not only from its usual winter of confined intensity and consolidation, but also it seems to be opening out to an even larger and more powerful cycle or vista of renewal. There is a sense that we're at the edge of a new phase, one that is clarifying our role and renewing the will and wisdom and grace in each of us. Our changes and challenges are, really, a microcosm of the larger changes taking place in our society and culture.

Don and his wife Joyce, long-time enthusiasts for what High Wind represents and soon to become community residents, express their own reason for supporting our work:

> In so many ways we note an accelerating rate in the desire of people all around us to explore, to learn, to better know who and what they really are. . . . Many are experiencing this desire of spirit as growth potential, ecology, holism, going back to the land and to more natural ways of living— or as the search for meaning through the many paths of mysticism and esoteric knowledge at the core of all great religions. Or maybe even as the yearning among peoples for greater self-destiny and personal responsibility. The list is long; the human greening of our planet is becoming varied and illuminating.
>
> The vision of High Wind, then, is truly grand, yet is shared in some way by probably most peoples on the planet at this time. We anticipate that the spirit we are all helping to create will take on stronger form by the day. As this happens, it will link us to the greater spirit that forms and strengthens throughout the planet, and we can expect changes within both humankind and the planet that will be gratifying beyond expectation.

June

In mid-June, we settled down after the enormous buildup and excitement of the two Lorian seminars. Lorian is a group whose wisdom and experience created the educational thrust at Findhorn, the renowned spiritual/ecological community on the North Sea coast in Scotland. We tapped into that wisdom and experience to guide us through our own early challenges; for two decades, their summer seminar at High Wind was a high point of our year.

We moved through the rest of summer and into fall following fairly normal work rhythms and cooling off in the pond most afternoons. Some of us took time to pick buckets of the black rasp-berries abundant in the back meadows, surrounded by a sea of laven-der bergamot and black-eyed Susans. Others went bird-watching or sketching. More and more we're making space to experience the extraordinary beauty and restorative powers of this land.

September

Sunlight sifts through the entry arch of Jim's graceful small dome, now designated as High Wind's sanctuary. It falls on a bowl of meadow flowers set in the center of the floor. Five of us sitting on mats this early morning are aware of the high-pitched cricket chatter outside, and then we drift into the silence of our private spaces.

Marcia, our resident artist, and I, with others on occasion, have been plastering and sanding in the "great hall" of the bioshelter. Instead of feeling driven by a seemingly endless chore, we get engrossed in throwing ideas back and forth while teetering on the

The three cement-covered, Styrofoam-block domes were created to extend our sleeping and meeting spaces.

tops of our ladders, gooping the ceiling. Then we stop to change the music tapes or try out a folk dance step we're learning. Or we drop our trowels and run out to the top of the hill to lie in the grass and watch the clouds for a while. When work time and play time become blurred, the spirit sings and fatigue and heaviness fade.

Most of the forty-plus varieties of herbs planted at the bioshelter have made it, in fact probably because they were protected through the drought and heat by the ragweed we so frantically worked to pull out. Hunting another use for nature's dividend, Marcia tried boiling up the ragweed for a dye for the fabrics she and Lorri are creating. She's experimenting with wild plants for various uses; one is an Indian remedy, a jewelweed tincture for wounds.

The west section of the coop houses several of the new craft activities. Two of Marcia's looms are already in operation, and the shelves are lined with rainbow spools of wool. When Lorri isn't insulating her new room in the barn or preserving veggies, she's brewing up another batch of beer on the stove, sewing up a storm, or talking about making a blanket out of cattail fuzz!

Lorri, who spends numerous hours nurturing our main garden

Gardener Lorri with lettuces

BETSY ABERT

area, writes of the biggest challenge in maintaining a truly organic garden—pest control:

> A good deal of time was spent researching alternatives to chemical pesticides. One of our chief objectives this season was to prevent the slug invasion that plagued us last year. Before planting, the garden was tilled and old mulching materials removed, exposing a sizable slug population. As each area of ground was bared, the ducks were ushered in to feast on the critters.
>
> Later on we laid cardboard strips around certain areas and daily hand picked slugs that were caught napping in the cool shade. As a final precaution, Bob dug a trench around the garden and lined it with wood ashes to serve as a physical barrier. Now, almost four months later, it appears our efforts were successful. Only a few slugs have been seen, and damage is minimal. . . .

Lorri discusses other problems and natural remedies, and then she concludes:

> Sometimes in the evening I stand on the slope overlooking the garden and wonder at the abundance of life before me. The birds join me, their songs strumming the breeze as monarchs and swallowtails dance from plant to plant. Many of the walkways are impassable, overgrown with plants eager to stretch out in the sun. . . .
>
> Surely a wonderful spirit exists here, a powerful yet gentle spirit nurtured by the loving care and energy of those whose lives have touched this place. So many of you have shared this garden with us, and now, together, we share our joy.

What's Really Important
1984

January

A burst of organizational activity was sabotaged periodically when winter revved up early in December. Nature seemed to catch us off guard deliberately, reminding us yet again of our dependence on the elemental forces, our smallness in the total picture. When we were whacked with subzero temperatures for relentless stretches (-26 degrees was a low), it was academic that driveways at the farm were blocked with blowing drifts because the cars were already frozen into silence. The farm group was literally marooned.

Nevertheless, Christmas found a festive crowd in the country, with extended families, including lots of young people. The crowd also included Joann, just back from Findhorn, who anchored our spiritual energy. Along with chopping wood and muttering incantations over dead batteries, there was cross-country skiing, a square dance, Yule baking, candle-making and weaving for holiday sales, and other group-inspired adventures.

While the woodstoves in the farmhouse and coop were going double time, it was discovered that in the bioshelter, though thermal storage and night curtains aren't yet in place, when the sun is shining, the building is warm and pleasant. Marcia reports that even in the bitterest period she didn't light fires during the day and was comfortable working at her loom in the great hall. This augurs well for the bioshelter's performance when its systems are all in place.

There's a reason for plants and creatures to rest in winter, and we're still learning that humans, too, must slow down. On top of recognizing this archetypal rhythm, High Wind has to remind itself that, especially in the country, it is definitely a seasonal being and we who do its work need time to reflect on where we've been and to dream of what's ahead. It's a chance to get reacquainted with ourselves and to store up energy and enthusiasm for our more public and strenuous summers.

The trick is to get survival needs squared away ahead of the deep freeze, and then to relax into stretches of hibernation for creative and re-creative activities.

Service to the whole remains the motivating driver. To me, this means to each other and the earth, for the highest good of all. It is a transcendent idea that lifts and pushes us beyond our individual selves. It reminds us to walk and feel in the shoes (or hoofs or bark) of all life we encounter, as well as to care for and respect ourselves as essential parts of that divine force.

June

I spoke recently of "significant changes gusting up" at High Wind. Carrying that analogy along, it seems not entirely accidental that the radical renovation we were performing on the farmhouse interior was accompanied by the awesome sixty-to-eighty mph gales that blasted Wisconsin in late April. One gust tore loose the top vents in the bioshelter greenhouse and blew out a knee-wall window. So fierce were the winds that we were thankful to be working indoors. It even became problematic to walk down the road from the bioshelter.

Someone joked that maybe there was a self-fulfilling prophesy at work and that we ought to think about changing our name. I prefer to remember we picked "High Wind" not just because of the exhilarating natural turbulence on the site, but also because we liked the symbolism of high energy and aspiration providing an impetus to pull us along and point us in directions that often we've understood only in retrospect.

Last night, as the High Wind Board sat discussing financial strategies in the farmhouse, somebody burst in with the urgent imperative: "No one leaves tomorrow without going to the woods to see the yellow lady slippers and wild geraniums!" Just to emphasize what's really important.

Lorri reports on garden activity:

The breath of spring blows across this land with great vigor, and with it we celebrate the glorious new season. As the first spears of asparagus pierce the light, we witness the rebirth and are reminded that the circle is truly unbroken.

I am drawn to the words of Alexander Pope: "Nothing is foreign; parts relate to the whole; One all-extending, all-preserving soul connects each being, greatest with the least; Made beast in aid of Man, and Man of beast; All served, all serving; nothing stands alone; the chain holds on, and where it ends, unknown."

It is in this spirit that our garden flourishes, and where all forms of life are interrelated. While a variety of seedlings (vegetables, herbs and flowers) wait to be planted into the rich soil, the farm community has been busily preparing the area. Chickens have been tilling up the soil in search of harmful insects and weed seeds. Bess, our cow, and the goats have contributed a sizable amount of organic fertilizer. Honeybees are keeping a close watch on the progress in anticipation of the sweet nectar that soon will be flowing. A wonderful variety of birds, too, have returned to the area, bringing melodies of spring.

Karina, our community fourteen-year-old, was inspired by the end of winter:

First the snow melted. Then came days and days of cold rain. Then the rain stopped, and after the chilled, windy days that followed, came spring. Not the official day, which was somewhere between the melting snow and rain, for we still had a sheet of ice on everything and school was canceled.

Now we're in the real spring. It envelops you as you walk out the door. You can hear it with the birds, smell it with the grass, taste it in the morning mist, see the opening of new life and everywhere feel the exciting vibrations of a changing pace. The earth has shaken off her blanket of snow and is beginning to get dressed. Granted, it took her long enough to get out of bed, but then not all of us wake up fast.

What wonderful clothes she is wearing! Every day a new flower appears, some expected, some not. While the new ones get special attention, the old ones are fondly greeted too.

During the June Lorian seminar: a full moon walk through the woods, feeling our way through dense brush. Trees sighing. Touching the bent oak. Emerging in the field, joining others at the fire circle. Marveling at the great white globe sailing in and out of swift clouds. Warm winds gusting.

Nature spirits in the garden: Dorothy Maclean and seminar-goers

September

Remembering the fall equinox celebration during the three-community seminar: In predawn darkness, everyone gathering slowly from the corners of the property, playing simple instruments. Mysterious flute sounds from the west meadow, an answer from the forest. Standing at the sacred circle to watch the red sun appear. More vigorous music now, spontaneous dancing around the flames. A tall altar of cornstalks and wind chimes silhouetted against the eastern sky. Ceremony and song. Tears.

An ethnobotany excursion with Lee Olsen. Standing in the fen beside Grandfather Birch, underground brooks gurgling out through tangled grasses, first hidden, then cascading into sand-bottomed pools. Learning that these precious, deep waterways are what keep the water pure for the entire surrounding region. At the moment Lee offers an Indian prayer, three low-flying geese suddenly skim the treetops. Sacred land!

Indian leader John Boatman and the sacred bent oak

October

Redwing blackbirds watch my progress through the wet meadow grass. Fence post sentinels, they're ushering me to the sanctuary this early morning. Stepping out of my boots, I stoop into the doorway to join the circle of silence with six others. When thoughts creep in, I notice that the wind speaks through the tall trees outside the dome, reminding me gently why I'm here: to listen and draw strength from the fundamental life forces.

Then a faint honking signals that the flight pattern of Canada geese heading south is bringing the flock directly overhead. The cacophony swells until it is momentarily deafening, then is gone. Interesting how we have to work at being constantly aware of the oneness, while the geese, and all other nonhumans, know so easily the natural rhythms and how all of creation fits together. I become even more conscious of how the power and beauty of this land invites love and gentleness among those who come here— and I give thanks.

Now, with the forests and fields turning golden, we begin to anticipate again our seasonal balancing. Marcia, who heard the geese with me in the sanctuary, was reminded of winter coming, the time of isolation and quiet introspection and personal creativity— so essential to offset the richness of many guests.

Lorri reflects:

> With the coming of autumn we celebrate the season of harvest. It's been a perfect summer in the High Wind garden, as evidenced by over 1,500 pounds of organically grown produce gathered. But the garden has provided us much, much more than food for our table.
>
> Through experiences here we're learning more about our relationship with Nature and gaining a deeper understanding and appreciation of the complex web of life. . . . A grassy plot toward the center was turned into a bird sanctuary with feeders, baths and a martin house. Inter-plantings of catnip

and borage attracted huge numbers of our honeybees, the latter playing an important part in pollination. Rock piles and watery areas bordering the garden provided habitat for beneficial garden snakes and toads.

We recognize the role these creatures play in Nature's design and welcome their presence.

Weeds, too, play an important part in the garden. Lambs quarters was allowed to grow wherever it wished as it attracted aphids and leaf miners away from our precious crops. A patch of deadly nightshade remained at the garden border to attract potato beetles. Another long patch of weeds and grasses, including goldenrod, ragweed, burdock, and pigweed, was left intact as habitat for beneficial insects. Pigweed was also left as a companion plant, particularly among root crops. Apparently this plant also helps to break up and improve the condition of the soil in general.

Rituals

1985

June

Springtime rituals. Full moon walk, sensuous fragrance of wild fruit blossoms exaggerated in the night air. Plunging into the hollow stillness of the forest, Keith leading and identifying the tall, mature canopy trees—the few spared in our relatively young woods: the great maples, oaks, ash, and hickory. Even elm bravely pushing up to full growth to replace dead grandfathers at whose skeletal feet we searched for the prized morel mushrooms sometimes found in these spots. So bright that, even in the deepest kettles, leaf shapes and plants stood out clearly, and the profusion of white trillium positively glowed.

We emerged from the damp recesses, climbed around the ghost of wigwam past, and out into the luminous meadow, its winter grasses whispering in the warm breeze. Watched the great globe ride in and out of low-flying clouds.

It was early May, and we were on one of several magical adventures during what was an unbelievable springtime for Wisconsin, going on for much of the previous month. The lilacs and honeysuckle in the yard all burst out ahead of schedule, their old-fashioned nostalgic scents mingling with those of their wild cousins in the meadows, lasting and lasting as if time itself had stopped.

One balmy night, sleeping bags were dragged to the hilltop and eyes propped open to watch the light show of the aurora borealis shimmering in the northern sky hour after hour.

Despite the devotion felt in pressing forward to complete the bioshelter, there have been moments snatched to let this incongruous heat seep into our pores, to smell the new life emerging from the ground, to spin gossamer dreams.

Even in the midst of a great deal of activity now at High Wind, I know the moments of absolute calm or transcendence are available. I can remember to step outside myself to connect with the countless forms of life around, all trying to get through, chattering in their own languages, jogging my inattention with their vivid colors and exquisite shapes, their perfumes; caressing with warmth and light, refreshing with a cooling breath. I can switch off my left brain, open my eyes and just be there with a universe that asks only to cooperate. Spring—a reminder to let go of old habits, to lift self-imposed blinders, to expand, to be drawn into the intricacies of the natural realm waking up, to remember to wake up with it.

Spring trillium blanket the forest floor; two small communitarians

"There is something truly magical about springtime in Wisconsin," observes Lorri. "Like the sap rising in the trees, we, too, are filled with new energy, drawn out of our winter hibernation to witness the season of rebirth. As the chives appear almost defiantly from beneath the snow, we know the gardening season, as well, is close at hand."

Last week, fourteen of us consecrated the fire circle with a Native American pipe ceremony. Carol Glover, a visiting workshop leader, welcomed the grandmothers and grandfathers from the four directions and from the sky and earth. We "smudged" ourselves and the hilltop by burning tobacco (sage) to cleanse and clear away the old energies and prepare for the new. Only then could we pass the lighted pipe around the circle, where we sat under the full moon, each drawing in the smoke and sending it out with our silent visions for the future, knowing also that once we had participated in this ceremony, we are always "in the pipe." Each time it is smoked, our thoughts and prayers will be heard and acknowledged.

Physicists teach us that everything is energy, vibrating at different rates. We're beginning to understand now, as did the mystics and Native Americans before us, that by shifting beliefs and attitudes, it is possible to change the vibrational rates of what we perceive, to alter our reality. This sense that we are participating in shaping a new world also harks back to the co-creative powers assumed by the early Celts and to their acceptance of the power and divinity present in all life. If we are to be custodians of our sacred land, we cannot afford to forget the old ways. We must honor the legacy of respecting and caring for each part of the Creation.

Does this mean, as well, that we approximate the life of those whose roots and vibrations permeated this farm for hundreds of years? Do we leave the land undisturbed so that perhaps the shades of all the beings that once shared this place will remain here in harmony with its new stewards? Is this a condition?

I believe High Wind can be a bridge between past and future. We can remember the wisdom of the old traditions, and we can also integrate new ways to express our connection with the earth, nature, the cosmos. It's a rather different world today. Not many of us can live lightly, dwelling in wigwams and hunting and gathering our food. Yet we're just beginning to understand and make use of technologies that work with the natural laws, that allow us to utilize energy that renews itself, ways of leaving a far less heavy footprint than have the boots we've been clumping around in over the past two centuries. Ways of building soil, not depleting it, constructing homes that can virtually maintain themselves.

Our bioshelters, our solar and earth-sheltered dwellings, may be the new wigwams. Our consciousness about waste and pollution may come in time to stem the mischief we've perpetrated so insanely.

If High Wind has one clear mandate, it is to join together the best and highest from the past with whatever embryonic clarity we can mobilize to carry us into a future worth living.

Kesha was a participant in our three-community seminar—a university credit program where students of all ages spent a month at High Wind, a month at Findhorn, and a month either

The High Wind bioshelter, a passive solar "micro farm"

at Sirius in Massachusetts or a community in the French Alps. During her High Wind stay, Kesha felt a profound connection with our land:

> The golden hours were fading as the sun slipped beyond the western ridge. Yet its brilliance lingered on, streaming iridescent amber light across the alfalfa fields. A hawk swirled in the shifting evening breeze, catching the fiery rays under her wing and casting them down with such force that I felt my eyes almost burned with the brightness. A part of me floated off with her as she circled out of sight and I questioned whether the vision was real. . . . I walked on among the changing faces of spring. Trilliums, in their final moments, spilled living white petals into a violet aura before returning their presence to the earth.
>
> As I approached the sacred oak, tremors of the encroaching night played on my eardrums. Bullfrogs and whippoorwills vibrated forcefully, offering a sound at once lonesome and communal. I saw the split limb lying on the ground and offered tobacco for the tree's shattered spirit. I could hear it speaking to me, crying out with a will to be heard:
>
> "I do not want to die on a land whose organizing powers do not remember the heritage here." The tone was despairing, yet the tree had let go of much of its pain in attempting to restore balance. In my attunement I received that it is essential we commit and deepen ourselves with the rhythms of the Mother as we continue to branch out to an extended family.

October

It wasn't until 1985 that Bel and I were finally able to start constructing our own solar house at High Wind. On a clear, hot August day, I watched the bulldozers making the first passes over the land where we were about to start building. After fifteen years of standing out on that hill that is now part of High Wind and imagining this moment, it was finally happening. More recently we'd been preparing the land and its inhabitants for the disturbances, asking the blessing of the small current residents and promising to be as careful and sensitive as we could in joining them in their space.

The cuts grew deeper, to bury the house as low as possible into the west hill, both to keep the profile unobtrusive from the nearby fire circle on top of the ridge and to shelter the house from the prevailing northwest winter winds. We wanted to emphasize the feeling that the house is growing organically out of the existing topography. Soon the site resembled an archeological dig, with the different levels of earth connected by ladders, and a fascinating geological history was spread out in the open cross sections. The glacial residue, or moraine, special to this area, consisted of layers of top soil, clay, packed round stones, fine pebbles, and beach sand, with the course of a long-ago stream clearly visible.

One of our objectives was that the house be "lyrical" and "knock-your-socks-off" aesthetically and at the same time feel understated, warm, and inviting—belying stereotypes of solar homes that are stark or ugly and scream "high-tech." More practically, we wanted to demonstrate an economy of scale and energy, to be comfortable without extravagance. We felt the architecture

RONALD M. OVERDAHL, *MILWAUKEE JOURNAL SENTINEL*

Bel and Lisa finally move into their own
solar house at High Wind.

was indeed dictated by the land, the spaces within evolving out of the natural flow and from the light patterns streaming in at various times of the day through many strategically placed windows.

Late one afternoon in September, I was leaning out of a window frame in the living room, touching in with the pungent dried meadow grasses and the eastern hills bathed golden by the reflected setting sun, and I was caught in one of those increasingly frequent moments of sensing a definite camaraderie with my house.

About a month ago, I suddenly realized that the building had ceased to be a creation simply willed into existence by a few people—it had become a being in its own right with its own personality of grace and beauty and power. It was taking its place as a working member among all the elements coming together to form an integrated community on this land—natural and human.

One of my own strategies when I feel overloaded and pressured is just to stroll out into our High Wind woods. Often it happens that where a particular intent or energy has been well grounded, where gentleness and caring have blessed the physical environment itself, a gift of healing is given back. It's as if the land is reminding me to stop and breathe deeply, to step out of my prickly human shell and into nature's aura of peace.

I'm invited to release the chatter in my head, the jockeying voices of self-justification or self-pity or self-blame. I'm pushed to make a space for the intelligence, whatever that may be, that over lights my life, to speak and work. I sense I can touch into an affection and encouragement that doesn't judge as I may judge myself. When I remember to be open, I'm "filled up." It seems to be a law of the universe. The scary voids vanish. It's as if a constant carrot were beckoning me to come to the secret, magic places, to remember what's really important—and then the strength and answers are there.

More simply, when I'm grumpy, I go for a walk. And even if I'm not, it's quite a wonderful way to spend an hour or two.

High Wind women at work: Lorri and Joann split and chop wood.

March

Joann reflects on a particularly fierce winter:

> The snow and cold temperatures came early, before we were psychologically or physically prepared for winter, and we've had continuous snow cover ever since. There's been digging out logs with crowbars and picks to cut and split for firewood (because we weren't prepared), cars too cold to start, shoveling out the driveway rapidly blowing shut, and an ice storm that brought down many branches around the farm.
>
> It's March now, and the small sanctuary dome is still very much not in evidence, being totally buried in snow. Through it all, the exquisite beauty of so much pristine snow cover drifting in unusual and fanciful patterns, remarkable crystalline structures grown overnight on window panes, prismatic displays of color on ice-laden trees catching the sun's rays, have worked their magic on our spirits.

Poems

1987

April

*J*just glanced out of our living room window to catch eight deer flying down the valley from the bioshelter hill. It's still awesome to wake up every day to this panorama that stretches east to Lake Michigan.

I love being able to go a few steps up to the fire circle to take part in an Indian balancing dance with flames crackling in the snow and the full moon sailing in and out of the mist. Or to take a breather from my desk to climb the fallen "magical tree" with my grandchildren, Lark and Niko. Or wade through the marshy turf in the fen and stretch out on the big warm rock.

Indian balance dance to all the directions

41

George Schricker sent us these poems after visiting High Wind:

Clearing the Path
All day
we work
in this garden.
Each stone we move,
moves us.
At the end of day
someone comes
to tell us
of supper.

Flute Song
      I know what notes
    are made of
   & how the wind
joins them all together—
      these birds
     & the fellow hammering,
     everything makes sense
when we are all together.

Tonight
the sun goes down
inside me,
stepping thru the door
into a field
of stars.

High Wind
I come here to kiss you
and you kiss back.

It's becoming easier to speculate that increasingly strange weather conditions are more than chance anomalies. In our own corner of Wisconsin, we can cite last summer's drought, then a bizarre ice sheet that covered the ground most of the winter, which resulted in instant lakes and torrents in our woods and fields when the snow began to melt and couldn't penetrate the frozen earth.

Yet after all that, as I write now, sitting at our new circle of sacred stones near the sweat lodge, the meadow grasses have never been so luxuriant, their waves of green rippling on this bright windy day in early June. Pale, tentative new leaves have deepened overnight to summer hue. The trillium, just finishing in the woods, have given way to the wild geraniums and hidden clumps of rare yellow lady slipper orchids. Drifts of indecently lovely white and pink blossoms—the hawthorns and wild fruit trees—delineate the hedgerows and forest edges.

How could it possibly be that all is not well? At a moment like this, it's easy to believe it's going to be "normal" after all. Who knows, with appreciation and caring poured from more and more of us toward our mother earth (on both the emotional and

John and Joann practice t'ai chi.

physical levels), we may yet be able to affect the seemingly inexorable roll toward self-annihilation.

Perhaps one of the most significant steps in building cohesion in the community was the dedication of the big dome as our permanent sanctuary. We held a very moving candle-lit meditation there for the spring equinox, and all decided on the spot that even though we're short on staff and guest living space, this building had finally realized its true function.

Interesting that a couple of days later the bizarre floods began, with a snowmelt runoff resulting in a roaring "mountain brook" in our woods, so loud you couldn't hear a shout ten feet away, and the just-sanctified dome became a lonely white island in a giant lake—the nearest approach point, fifteen feet away. We pondered the meaning of our newly precious sanctuary sitting for the first time in two feet of water!

Blessed to Be Here

1989

Spring/Summer

Louise, newly arrived to live at High Wind, shares:

Yesterday I walked to our newest sacred circle at the edge of the woods near the hermitage. I was alone, so I had my "deer ears" on—listening for birds, trees, grass and critters. I heard footsteps in the dead leaves that sounded like a four-legged, so I stopped. Not having the patience of a deer, I waited a few minutes, listening to the birds and trees, and then went on.

As I approached the clearing with the sweat lodge and fire circle in front of me and the sacred circle and sun to my left, I heard and then saw the deer. They were just on the other side of the clearing. I wasn't aware of them until they moved, so I didn't see their sweet faces, only their white tails. I sat near the fire circle for a long time then, feeling the sun on my back . . . and my connection with the earth. The deer were not far away; I could occasionally hear them move through the dead leaves in the woods.

I am blessed to be here. When I can have the experience of wholeness that being close to the earth gives me, I function better in all environments. Not that my transition to High Wind has been totally smooth; all transitions are scary, exciting, difficult and new. But I am here!

Playing by Nature's Rules
1989–1990

Fall/Winter

Jan, a High Wind resident, tells how she relates to the land:

> The woods at High Wind are a magical place. If you wander off the paths you can wade through piles of crackling leaves. Then lie on your back and take time to be very, very quiet. If you listen, you can hear the trees talking about autumn, about death and the cycle of winter into spring and rebirth. They can take your fear away . . . and replace it with a boldness that makes life a grand adventure.

It seems one simply doesn't have time to pause and wonder what impact our actions are having on the "lesser" life forms. It's certainly an awareness that the land of High Wind seems to invite: lying eye to eye with a busy spider in the tall grasses; watching a water lily long enough in the early morning to see it unfold its white petals to the sun; noting with satisfaction that what was a small patch of wild bergamot last year has multiplied and spread over a considerable portion of the meadow; identifying the well-mashed paths of the deer in their regular trek through the woods down to the fen for water. Just slowing down to watch and delight in the abundances of nature in motion. Something is always dappling in the sunlight, rippling with the wind, shining, and driven by the rains.

Toward midnight on an early September evening, Don phoned. "It's starting!" he shouted.

As a night person and regular watcher of the heavens, Don keeps track of events like an aurora borealis. Bel and I dashed out to the top of our hill to see the pale green and pink fingers of light flickering more and more boldly up over our woods to the north. The night was crystalline and still, and we found we could talk in conversational voices to Don way up next to his house, and to Ray, watching nearly a quarter of a mile away near the farmhouse.

Magical! But isn't it all. . . .

Spring/Summer

Nature's clock went a little crazy this year, with several unprecedented days in the steamy 90s in April, followed in May by eight inches of snow. Spring has come in fits and starts. From down-jacket walks in our muddy brown woods with piles of snow still hiding on the north sides of the bare trees, suddenly the new green haze is everywhere. Marsh marigolds in dazzling, yellow profusion, showcased against the black gurgle of Nichols Creek. Green poking up through bleached winter field grasses, and red-winged

Ice storm: crystal magic

blackbirds trilling their throats out as they swoop between old mullein stalks.

Behind the thoughts of the obligations of all peoples remains the cognizance that we will be able to continue playing out our brief human lives only if we agree to play by nature's rules of balance and respect. Standing in the morning stillness and looking out over the tender greens coming to life in our valley, I think about the quote Marcia recalled the other day: "Every time we step on the earth, imagine that we are stepping on the belly of a pregnant woman." The degree to which we acknowledge our responsibility to both great planetary trends *and* minute daily happenings will determine the shape of our future.

I happened to glance up at the row of giant sentinel oaks guarding the forest edge and watched a squirrel race up a nearby trunk. At the tip of the still-bare crown, he decided he wanted to reach the last tree down the line. We clumsy humans would have had to clamor down eighty feet and beat our way overland through tangled brush, but this small savvy fellow was admirably designed to expedite the process. He simply stuck his tail out

Field of chicory at High Wind with Springdale Farm below

behind for balance and literally flowed like water, straight as an arrow, across the highest branches from one tree to the next. He never paused or jumped but became a fluid, graceful stream that shot two hundred horizontal feet in considerably less than ten seconds.

I Am a Villager Now
1991

Fall/Winter

*I*n early December, having just returned from a study trip to Europe, I walked our country road, remembering the sea crashing against the cliffs on which the nearly inaccessible thirteenth-century Italian town of Manarola is impaled. I recalled the soaring topography of Liechtenstein, the tiny country where no fields are flat enough to cultivate. I remembered how each isolated hamlet we visited carried its own flavor, how the villagers spoke with a clear sense of identity and ease and pride in belonging to their respective communities.

It was a few days after a fury of winds from the northeast had sent us a blizzard of such intensity that snow was driven through the "breathing" cracks in our barn. Now the air was absolutely still, with even a promise and smell of spring warmth to come. Standing field corn furrowed with snow was glazed by the late afternoon sun. Dark evergreen stands cast long shadows. The huge red globe caught briefly in the web of naked branches bristling along the western hills—then dropped, and soon I had difficulty spotting the aluminum cans I was picking up from the roadside.

As the European villagers have a comfortable sense of belonging in their communities, so, too, am I a villager now. This is my home and I feel deeply peaceful here. I'm aware of the bridge I've made from my own European roots in towns like those we saw to the groupings that sprouted on the wide plains and glacial hills of the American Midwest. Here is the land we've been given to steward. This is our place in the world, our base, and it's from here that we are working and growing.

Just as I as an individual can't relate effectively to others until I'm at ease within myself, so it follows that the sense of security that comes from an identity with place is perhaps a prerequisite for identifying with the world community.

Our history at High Wind is *a little* shorter than that of the hill towns of Italy or the republics of the former Soviet Union, but the analogy works. Out of such strength and richness it is fitting for those of us so blessed to take a stand in remembering our place in nature's grand scheme—the biggest community of all—and the responsibility that goes with our unique gift among all the species: that of choice. Let us choose life and sanity and gentle consideration for all our fellow travelers on this earth.

Jan muses:

> Picture this—it's a warm day in late winter. The old snow and frozen grass stems are dissolving into a silvery slush underfoot. The willows are just beginning to shine with their springtime gold, and if you look carefully at the maples, they seem to be surrounded by a pale pink glow. All the gnarled bare old trees run the risk of looking a little silly in these subtle pastels—the understated colors of swelling buds and living bark. The first quickenings of spring are just this moment becoming apparent to the most patient and discerning eye.
>
> You hold your breath and realize that your mind has just created a hologram, swallowed this moment whole. Years and years from now, whenever you wish, perhaps on your deathbed, you will be able to step into this moment and experience it fully—the subtle colors, the smells, the exhilaration of returning life. This moment and eternity snap together neatly, forming a perfect sequence.

During a High Wind women's retreat last summer that focused on the life and pictorial illuminations of the twelfth-century mystic

Hildegard of Bingen, participants looked deeply at examples of Hildegard's symbolic art pinned up around the bioshelter seminar room. We allowed particular images to draw us, and we connected with them.

This was my experience: I wandered around the room peering at Hildegard's illuminations, and at one point my bare toes closed over one of the river stones in the floor—the perfect size to fill the hollow between my toes and the ball of my foot—cool, then warm and soft, an exact fit.

There was the instant flash that Eric, my son who had lived in the bioshelter and created a winding stonework "river" to soak up the sun's heat, had placed this stone, chosen it and lovingly sealed it in place to bring beauty to this room. In a very tactile way I was connecting with his love and creativity. The fact of giving birth and nurturing was turning around, and what he had given birth to was now giving back to me—giver and receiver, reversing and blurring.

I looked up at the illumination in front of me as my foot closed around the stone. The picture was a wheel with young men around it digging in the earth and planting trees. Eric is a landscape gardener/artist.

Prairie gold

Circles, connections; no head, no foot, no higher nor lower; no creator-created, no parent-child. Any or either one a hologram for the other, for the all.

No roles, all roles, interchanging roles. Intergenerational, mutually respecting, being open to the subtle shifting of configurations, noticing whatever seems to be. Spirit, or profound intelligence, at work.

Spirit moving in and through me.

Be still. Just watch it. Trust. Move.

Fresh Winds

Winter/Spring 1992

*W*e had just announced that after twelve years we were letting go of our identity as a tight-knit, "intentional" community. We all realized we were entering a new cycle that was pushing us to cut free and become simply a more relaxed "eco-neighborhood" of good friends.

As if to remind us that winds blow indiscriminately over everyone, and that one can never afford complacency, in mid-March we were snapped out of weeks of unprecedented mild weather when, complacently, we were expecting for once to drift into a gentle spring. (Spring is almost an unknown season in Wisconsin.)

In one day, the temperature dropped 50 degrees while we were pounded first by a deluge of rain, then sleet (accompanied eerily by thunder and lightning), then glare ice everywhere, followed by a driving blizzard.

Three days after the March snow, Bel and I hiked coatless across the meadow into the state forest under a hot sun and cobalt sky, noisy winds blowing away the remaining storm clouds and tearing off last winter's dead oak leaves to make space for the new buds. Honking formations of Canada geese winging north reminded us that life is made up of cycles and that what is good will endure and what is not will give way to something more viable than the old.

Autumn 1995

Although we've relinquished the intentional community, High Wind continues its schedule of educational offerings. Visitors come to participate in programs, yet consistently they find that shifts in perception result as much from their encounter with the land as from new ideas. They wander in the peaceful meadows and woods, they climb to the hilltops for dramatic vistas, or they're drawn to musical brooks edged with wild watercress.

Over and over we're reminded that, beyond anything we might teach or build on our 292 acres, nature herself offers infinite gifts— the chance to let go, to connect with spirit, to heal, to gain fresh perspective, to see truly.

Spring 2000

Last summer was verdant, slow-moving. We in the High Wind Learning Community (which has taken the place of the residential community) gathered often to indulge in luminous conversations and to post dreamy scenarios on the ethereal web. Then, with the crisping of autumn, the clouds of pale yellow butterflies disappeared. Winter was upon us, and suddenly we woke up to the sharp reality that a long, familiar chapter in our life and work was closing and that a new one is being written. On the "campus," just as the fresh spring winds are beginning to blow and a warmer sun is coaxing new life from our brown meadows and bare trees, so, too, the curtain is rising on High Wind's next act.

Eric built a boardwalk to span the soggy fen.

Earth Messengers
Echoes from the Past

*T*he bird sounds at High Wind frequently carry me back to shadowy, delicious remembrances from my earlier life. They stand out as points of stillness when I am truly at peace, in equilibrium—when my usual darting, worrying, anticipating mind goes quiet. I'm filled up with the moment's sensations, which shut out any disturbing urgencies.

The flute of the wood thrush, floating up from the kettles, conjures up a field trip into the woods of northern New Jersey with my third-grade teacher (the one who let me skip arithmetic lessons in order to write a story or poem, usually about nature). I'm transported back to that dark glen of damp earth, mosses, and ferns; I smell them and feel embraced in the magic of great towering trees.

An early sun is just clearing the eastern horizon as I hang out the wash on my High Wind hillside. Only the muffled cooing of a mourning dove breaks the silence. The earth strains to warm around me—a blessed warming, so different from the ominous human-induced heating-up being reported. . . .

One of my great pleasures is remembering early mornings (undoubtedly Mondays) in our yard in Connecticut when I was growing up, helping my mother hang the laundry. I remember heavy dew still glistening in the grass and that same utter quiet, broken only by the occasional soft call of a mourning dove. I'm watching my mother shaking out, then gathering up the corners of the sheets, showing me how to pin them.

When I hang out my wash now, invariably I'm back in Connecticut, reenacting this ancient female ritual. And often the mourning dove is calling hauntingly to remind me. Is my mother there too?

I'm off on my daily walk up the road and it's slightly foggy. There's no wind. No tree branches, no tawny, dried grasses stir. The air is moist and pleasantly warm. Lately there's been a cacophony of excited birds gathered in certain trees, maybe newly returned from the South. Or the odd blackbird is trilling its heart out on the electric wires overhead, and its friend is answering from a nearby perch.

But then, all of a sudden, there's absolute silence. Nature is holding its breath. Everything stops. There's the strange sensation in my ears I get when there's a complete absence of sound, almost as though they're plugged, or I'm aware of blood pumping or flowing. Then, out of the stillness, comes the quiet, lonely coo of a dove. I smile, because this is the sound, the bird, that triggers such a cascading flood of memories, of nostalgia. It's the song that immediately conjures up images of my mother and a simpler era.

Then there's the strident cry of the blue jay. I'm immediately back many decades, taking brisk autumn walks with my father and our family through woods and brambly fields and hills. The air is bracing, the sky clear blue, the leaves orange and red. His contagious excitement at just being "outdoors" and hiking hard and purposefully catches each of us. For some reason, the jay evokes my father's spirit that loved to explore "the wild" so intensely that when I hear the cawing now, I find myself silently acknowledging my father's presence.

I sense he may be dipping into my life to remind me of the caring that he couldn't express verbally but that imprinted itself in a legacy of this love affair with nature that he passed on to me (and to my brother and my two sons). That he got from his father and his grandfather, a noted botanist.

The robin. Her quiet song transports me to long-ago memories of dusk falling over a freshly mown, sweet-smelling lawn that stretches down a long slope; there are showy white and pink peonies spilling over their beds. There's a stillness, the resting reward at the end of the day. The unassuming little chirp sets the perfect tone for this quiet scene. It's also the first bird out in the morning, urgently heralding the dawn, somehow reminding me of less complex times when unformed images of family life and places of home held me in protective arms.

Mostly feelings, rather than distinct pictures, are evoked that are steadying, that bring flashes of momentary delight and well-being. As if the influence and caring of family were still being projected through these humble bird messengers.

A walk through the cathedral of tall pines and spruce arching over the path to the old sweat lodge site calls up another woods walk thirty years ago in Scotland. It was during my first visit to Findhorn and involved my eerie connection with one tree in that woods. Here's how I described it in my journal:

> I hesitate to include this next experience—not being quite sure what it meant, not wanting to attach to it an exaggerated importance—nor to further strain the credulity of readers. Yet, it happened and is part of the total picture. Some visitors come to Findhorn determined to feel devic (angelic) energies, to see evidence of nature spirits, to find their own miracles. I didn't think I had this kind of sensitivity and made no effort to "look."
>
> One afternoon when a group went off to Randolph's Leap with community member Dick Barton to meditate under what he said was a particularly powerful tree, I went along, mainly to enjoy this incredible spot with great conifers, silver beeches, and russet forest floor. We sat in silence for an hour in the cold (and light rain) under this two-hundred-foot-tall fir with a mammoth trunk. Then, still in silence, we drove the eight miles back to Findhorn. I had felt nothing unusual.

A week later I was back in the forest climbing over the rocks with a friend, and as we were leaving, I mentioned that there was a special tree. Did he want to see it? We leaned against opposite sides of the tree and closed our eyes. I began to experience a strange sensation: of being pulled into the center of the great trunk and then stretching higher and higher till I was as tall as the tree. I became very giddy and had the feeling that if I opened my eyes I'd be peering way, way down to see my feet tiny and distant below in the fallen leaves.

We moved away from the tree simultaneously ten minutes later, and when I told my companion what had happened, his mouth dropped open.

"But that's exactly what I experienced too. And with my eyes shut I was 'seeing' out in front of me, through the tops of the beech and fir branches, to a dense stand of evergreens several miles across. Beyond the wood there was a shining body of water."

There was no way he could have known what lay off to the north; we'd come in from the west. Now, leaving, we drove north and came to an extensive pine plantation, a national forest. And, once on the other side, we arrived at the shore of the Moray Firth.

It's March and we're burning the prairie in front of the bioshelter. Armed with shovels, a group of High Winders watches the slow creep of flames westward from the fire lane we've carefully prepared to nudge the burn in the right direction. Suddenly the wind flares up and reverses, the fire jumping the burned lane and racing in the opposite direction. We manage to stop it, but not before it takes out several bushes we'd planted.

I'm reminded of the days in Connecticut when my little brother and I and a few neighbor kids were drafted to monitor the burning of our two-acre field every summer. My mother, ordinarily quite courageous, would retreat into the house, too frightened by big fires even to watch. My father was in his element, though, and when the leaping flames occasionally spread out of control, beyond what we could beat down easily with our shovels, the thrill of danger, of risk, was what made the day for him. (I don't recall that the volunteer fire department had to be summoned more than once.)

Those were the same fields where, every August, we hired a

1940: Neighbors gather to burn our Connecticut field.

1941: Haying with draft horses

fellow teenager, Hank Lent, to come down the hill with his prized team of draft horses and wagon to cut the hay for my goats. (I raised and milked three goats, and my brother had responsibility for a flock of chickens for the "war effort." And, of course, we grew a Victory Garden and foraged for dandelion greens, fiddle-heads, blueberries, and other wild edibles.)

Drifting off to sleep on our screened porch at High Wind, the soft afternoon breezes are blowing in all the delicious perfumes of mid-May blossoms: Russian olives, the wild fruit trees, dogwood, my Daphne bush and—most powerfully—several giant lilacs, now heavy with purple and white clusters. It's said that smells are what evoke past experiences most sharply, and I think, for me, it's the lilacs that conjure up one of my clearest and most treasured memories.

This one goes back over sixty years, during World War II. I was in the eighth grade and, miracle of miracles, a full-blown crush on a classmate was actually reciprocated. Bill, the son of a

Lisa Paulson with goat kids, circa 1942

well-known foreign correspondent, and his parents had recently escaped just ahead of the Nazi invasion of France, so he was already surrounded by a romantic aura and, although American, he spoke with a faint French accent and also looked a bit like a young Laurence Olivier.

It was the spring of 1942, and Bill used to bike the ten miles across our rural Connecticut town to my house. At dusk, two very shy and totally inept thirteen-year-olds would stroll down Lyons Plains Road, holding hands and struggling to overcome the fact that we were both painfully challenged in the conversation department. Not that that mattered. A looming, shadowy hedge of lilac bushes enveloped us in their strong sweet scent, magnified by the rising damp of the night. Volumes of unspoken poetry, two hearts pounding. . . .

Ever since, lilacs in May work their magic like clockwork, and I'm once again that awkward eighth grader in the throes of her First Love—breathless, embarrassed, ecstatic.

Quiet Waters

Coda

*I*n 2001, we began to transfer ownership to two Buddhist groups, one Tibetan-based and the other with Japanese Zen roots. Windhorse, the Tibetan group, acquired our bio-shelter and then, in 2007, the west meadows and woods. High Wind is collaborating with Windhorse to establish the Midwest Shambhala Retreat Center. This center is dedicated to meditation, peace, and sustainability. High Wind continues to host and advise visiting educators and environmentalists and has established a foundation to provide leadership and financial support for sustainability initiatives throughout the region.

Here is an excerpt from the book that I wrote to document the history of High Wind. I felt it appropriate to conclude *Voices from a Sacred Land* with these images, as they highlight the power of our land and the forces of nature.

> This brings the saga of High Wind up to date. The history stands firm, the mantle is now shared, and the twenty residents—including community veterans, several more recent homeowners, and the Buddhist newcomers—are coexisting gracefully, getting together for occasional potlucks, house concerts, walks in the woods, and to exchange books, DVDs, good conversation, and more. We watch out for each other as we also happily "do our own thing."
>
> All of us are held in the loving embrace of our enchanted, healing land, the carpet of white trillium under the oaks and maples in May, the fiery golds and scarlets of

autumn, waist-high grasses and wildflowers in the summer meadows, the quiet black and white forest of winter.

And then there is the *wind*—so often the wind. The freight train roar that begins in the deep glacial kettles at the bottom of our woods, accelerating until it bursts from the trees. Updrafts that toss billowy thunderheads across an August sky and give the circling redtails a free glide. Gale forces from the east that send February blizzards howling across the spine of our high, open ridge so fiercely that we can barely stand.

And then a gentle sighing among the towering pines on the path to the hermitage. . . . Wind is the signature energy that has carried those stewarding these High Wind lands for the past quarter century. Now its new custodians are charged to ride it into the future.

I conclude with the High Wind credo that, over and over through the years, drew us back to our central purpose and that, with great satisfaction, we passed on to the Windhorse folks:

> To *walk gently on the earth,*
> To *know the spirit within,*
> To *hear our fellow beings,*
> To *invoke the light of wisdom, and*
>
> To *build the future now.*

DOUG GREEN

. . . so often the wind

About the Author

Writer and artist Lisa Paulson grew up along the East Coast of the United States. In 1952, with backpack and idealism, she landed in South Italy, where she was to live off and on for the next nine years. In Naples, Lisa met and worked with Belden Paulson, who had created Casa Mia, a settlement center for homeless Neapolitans displaced by World War II. The couple married in 1954. In the fall of 1957, Lisa, Bel, and their eleven-month-old son Eric returned to Italy to spearhead a project to resettle Iron Curtain refugees on the island of Sardinia. They remained in Sardinia for two years and then moved to Rome, where Bel worked with the United Nations to implement a plan to resettle the remaining refugees in Italian camps. While in Rome, their son Steven was born. The family moved to Wisconsin in the fall of 1962.

Between 1976 and 1998, Lisa made a number of extended visits to the Findhorn Foundation, the renowned community modeling new ways of living near Inverness in northeast Scotland. These visits, along with her travels to the New Alchemy Institute in Massachusetts, had a profound impact on the creation of High Wind, an intentional community she and Bel founded in the early 1980s. High Wind, a small, rural enclave abutting the Northern Kettle Moraine State Forest in Wisconsin, focused on matters of ecology, education, and spirit.

It was at High Wind that Lisa came to cherish even more deeply the central role of the natural world. Not only did nature here clearly influence the lives of High Wind's residents, but Lisa recognized that throughout her own life, the poetry and power inherent in certain landscapes have shaped her beliefs, her passions, and her pursuits.

Currently, Lisa and Bel divide their time between the country-sides of Wisconsin and Vermont.

Coming Home